John Mole was born in Somerset in 1941, and now lives and works in Hertfordshire. He has published several collections of poetry and, as a broadcaster, has compiled and presented feature programmes for BBC radio. He also plays regularly as a jazz clarinettist. John Mole is married to the artist Mary Norman. They have two sons.

# John Mole
## *Back By Midnight*

*Illustrated by Peter Bailey*

**PUFFIN BOOKS**

PUFFIN BOOKS

Published by the Penguin Group
Penguin Books Ltd, 27 Wrights Lane, w8 5tz, England
Penguin Books USA Inc., 375 Hudson Street, New York, New York 10014, USA
Penguin Books Australia Ltd, Ringwood, Victoria, Australia
Penguin Books Canada Ltd, 10 Alcorn Avenue, Toronto, Ontario, Canada m4v 3b2
Penguin Books (NZ) Ltd, 182–190 Wairau Road, Auckland 10, New Zealand

Penguin Books Ltd, Registered Offices: Harmondsworth, Middlesex, England

Published in Puffin Books 1994
10 9 8 7 6 5 4 3 2 1

The poems in this volume have previously appeared in *Boo to a Goose* (1987) and
*The Mad Parrot's Countdown* (1990) by John Mole, published by Peterloo Poets

Poems copyright © John Mole, 1987, 1990
This selection copyright © Penguin Books Ltd, 1994
Illustrations copyright © Peter Bailey, 1994
All rights reserved

The moral right of the author has been asserted

Typeset by Datix International Limited, Bungay, Suffolk
Printed in England by Clays Ltd, St Ives plc
Filmset in Monophoto Baskerville

# Contents

## A Riddle

I am an instrument, a pipe,
A bright brass concertina
Making heavenly music.
Planets, spheres, the Plough, the Milky Way
All come at my calling
Winking at me, eye to eye,
As if they knew that he who plays me well
Will understand them, entering
The mystery of the universe and bringing closer
Infinite secrets held for aeons
In the darkness which I penetrate.

Play me in silence, and I'll give you
Silence in return
Though in your head, professor,
You'll be seeing stars.

# The Boy and the Sky

At his grandfather's house, at the top of the stairs
A small round window looked out on the sky;
It was empty, awful, a circle of nothing,
A transparent lid which blurred when the rain came
Or dazzled with sunlight, a frame but no picture;
It felt like a gap in the roof of his head,

And a curious buzzing began in his head
As he reached (past his bedtime) the foot of the stairs
Too afraid to go up; 'Oh you do look a picture'
His grandmother chuckled 'Afraid of the sky?
A brave boy like you?' Then his grandfather came
So he tried hard to tell him – got told it was nothing.

They didn't agree on the nature of nothing;
He couldn't explain; 'Don't go stuffing your head
With such nonsense' his grandfather ordered 'You

came

For a holiday. Buck up, enjoy yourself!' 'But it's the

stairs,

It's the stairs!' he insisted 'They go to the sky
Through that window. There isn't a picture

Like downstairs.' He thought of the picture
He saw from the living-room – that wasn't nothing
But something he knew about, putting the sky
In its place above landscape, a pattern, his head
Could make sense of it, not above stairs.
Again he looked up and the buzzing came

Louder, electric, like energy, came
And possessed him – the living-room picture
Clicked off and, abandoned, he charged up the stairs
Like a madman, his mind full of nothing,
Transparent and circular, threw back his head
As he ran and made mouths at the sky

While his grandparents watched him – 'It must be the
                                                      sky.
Quick, the poor child's not well!' So the doctor came
Grumbling and made him say 'Ah', then he nodded
                                           his head
Saying 'Why did you bother me? This boy's the
                                         picture
Of health, he'll grow out of it. Really, it's nothing
But fantasy, just like the Man on the Stairs.'

'But it's *not*, it's the sky! There isn't a picture!'
The boy wept with rage when they came saying
                                       'Nothing,
The doctor said', patted his head and went quietly
                                       downstairs.

# The Trick

One night, when I couldn't sleep,
My dad said
*Think of the tomatoes in the greenhouse*

And I did.
It wasn't the same as counting sheep
Or anything like that.

It was just not being in my room forever
On a hot bed
Restless, turning and turning,

But out there, with the patient gaze of moonlight
Blessing each ripe skin
And our old zinc watering-can with its sprinkler,

Shining through a clear glass pane
Which slowly clouded over into
Drowsy, comfortable darkness

Till I woke and came downstairs to breakfast
Saying *Thank you, Dad,*
*I thought of them. It did the trick.*

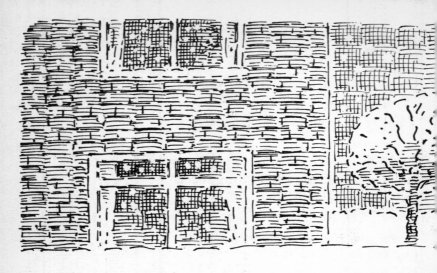

## *First Snow*

Whose is this long, unexpected elbow
Resting its white sleeve on the wall?
Is anyone out there when I call
To hear my voice? I've lost my echo.

Whose are those feathery tears that keep coming?
Somebody weeps without a sound
And leaves his grief heaped up on the ground.
It's so quiet my ears are drumming.

Whose is that handkerchief on the gatepost
Large enough for a giant sneeze?
*Bless you* whisper the shivering trees
While I just stand here like a ghost.

Who am I? And where have I woken?
It wasn't the same when I went to bed.
I still feel me inside my head
Though now a different language is spoken.

Suddenly all the meanings have gone.
Is someone trying to tell me something?
A bird shakes silver dust from its wing
And the sky goes on and on and on.

# A Ghost Story

When you come home and it's raining
And there's nobody in
And the kettle's switched off but still steaming
And the biscuit tin
Is full of biscuits (your favourite kind)
And the beds have been made
And you look in the fridge and you find
Everything splendidly arrayed
For your best meal ever but when you call
Nobody answers and even the cat
(Who doesn't like rain) is not in the hall
Or the kitchen or upstairs or anywhere at all
And there's no message left on a table or the doormat
And the damp patch seems to have grown larger on
                                            the wall
Then you have to admit it at last – you're afraid
No not that they've gone and left you behind
But that you yourself have been delayed
And that somehow someone broke into your mind
Before you got home, that you'll have to begin
All over again, that you've woken from dreaming
And nothing has changed except nobody's in
(Not even the cat) and it's still raining.

# Song for an Abandoned House

The glass is never mended,
The trees are always bare,
The sky is open-ended,
The end is open air,
The prospect is heart-broken,
The curtains will not close,
The truth remains unspoken,
The rest is not repose.

The rooms have been vacated,
The lock has turned its key,
The ghosts are reinstated,
The mirror cannot see,
The silence darts for cover,
The echo finds its voice,
The shadows haunt each other,
The house is spoilt for choice.

# *The Toy Squirrel's Lament*

It's bad enough
To be stuffed
But it feels
Even worse on wheels.

## Some Riddles

1
In the beginning
I became a wheel
And held enchantment
In my magic circles.

Then I became
The shape of order:
Spellbound citizens
Began to dream –

They dreamed their cities,
Pavements, statues;
Often I found my place
In one of those.

Paper may wrap me
But I blunt your scissors.
Heartless, my heart
Breaks many others.

2
Face to face or on the sly
I catch you with my sudden eye
And cannot, so they tell me, lie.

But when I let you reappear
Exactly as you were, oh dear,
The things you say, the things I hear:

'That's awful, that is really bad.
Do I always look so sad?
A cheat, a frame-up! I've been had.'

Oh thinning hair, oh broken tooth;
No one can give you back your youth.
How inconvenient the truth.


3
Who, sir, am I?
For a start, I hate sunshine
And deserve the penalty –
To be swallowed with good wine.
Miserable slitherer,
Landlubberly crustacean;
The French eat me, sir.
They are a wise nation!

## 4

Makeshift in Caesar's tent, I bore the weight
Of continents spreadeagled for his taking.

Courtly tales were told about my virtuous knights
But no one's perfect, and their King died broken-
                                    hearted.

Alexander, Charlemagne, a league of nations –
To and fro across me; treaties, bargains . . .

Empires pass; I watch them rise and fall,
A meeting of the board then liquidation.

As for you, you take your elbows off me.
Learn good manners and respect great men.

5

The nastier the day
The nicer we are to know;
We're a kind, you might say,
Of aerial raincoat
Or a rooftop on the go
Or even, stretching it,
The back of a duck.

Some of us will almost fit
Your pocket. Others
Can bring bad luck.

Whatever the time and place,
We're an open or shut case.


6

Through a bright autumnal air
We fall from grace, and from
The arms that held us.

The brilliant discourse of our veins
Has ended now; our fresh green thoughts
Must gossip with the dead ideas
Of yesterday.

Strewn, we lie at your feet
And when disturbed by shuffling children
Know that even they shall not escape.

7

The Romans built me straight.
They knew where they were going.
I am the quickest route there is
Unless the flies are crowing.

They say, when I lead to hell,
That I'm paved with good intentions.
I have known four strong legs give way
To fast four-wheeled inventions.

I'm what your cheery friend
Says 'Come on, let's have one' for;
And, I'm afraid, if your luck's running out,
When you reach my end you're done for.


8

Children used to give us to their teacher,
Rosy baubles shining on her desk,
And still, some say, we keep away the doctor –
Hardly science, but how picturesque.

# A Painting Lesson

(from the studio of Benjamin Mole)

Henri de Toulouse Lautrec
Couldn't paint to save his neck –
'Bring me a model!' he'd exclaim,
Swigging brandy from his cane,
'One of those fagged-out, scrawny dollies
That kick their legs up at the *Folies*.'
Then he'd dash off a few quick strokes
(A habit with those famous blokes
Who're reckoned to be good at art
But never finish what they start)
And all his fans would say 'Bravo!
Go on, have another go' –
Which Henri did; he squeezed those tubes
And painted ladies with big boobs
And gentlemen with silly hats
And dogs which looked much more like cats
And posters for the Music Hall
(Lousy paintings one and all)
And no one told him 'They'd be nicer,
Henri, if they were PRECISER'
But *I'd* have told him, I'd have said
'Come on, Henri boy, instead
Of all those smears and dots and dashes
Get yourself some fine, thin brushes,
Get your models from the shelf
In a proper model shop – an elf,
An orc, an ogre or a dwarf,
A snotling, ratman, even a smurf

Would be far better than *your* type, oh
Why not try a Mutant Psycho;
Beastmen, Chaos Knights and dragons
Are much more interesting than flagons,
Coffee cups and knives and forks
And all that restaurant rubbish! Orcs
Are in and Paris out,
War Games are what it's all about,
Painting armour really neat –
So give yourself a birthday treat.
Buy me a model. Let's have some fun,
And watch me show you how it's done!'

# First Fruit

Plucking a globe
From its living thread,
*Light is orange*
The painter said

Then considered this wasn't
For him to say,
Pocketed it
And walked away.

# The Goldfish

Through the ice swept clear of snow
There suddenly appeared a glow,

A glow of orange, then a glower,
A gaping, vacant-featured flower,

A flower which floated up, a face
Against the limits of its space,

Its space I gazed at vacantly,
As distant as eternity,

Eternity, unnumbered years
Of thought which comes then disappears,

Then disappears, a guilty wish,
As quickly as that flowery fish,

That flowery fish which turned about,
Flickered, dimmed and then went out,

Went out like a fading light
Into the darkness, far from sight,

From sight, but never far from mind,
Leaving its after-glow behind,

Behind, before, just once, not twice,
No second glances through the ice.

## The Call

You didn't answer when I called
Although I knew you must have heard.
Why was I suddenly appalled?
You didn't answer. When I called
The space between us was enthralled
And something in my memory stirred.
You didn't answer when I called
Although I knew you must have heard.

Why did you never call me back
Or let me know you'd changed the game?
Across our net's deceptive slack
Why did you never call me back?
Had I somehow lost the knack?
Were you really not to blame?
Why did you never call me back
Or let me know you'd changed the game?

# The Smile

It began with a whisper
But grew and grew
Until I felt certain
The source must be you.
Why did you smile
While I listened and then
Turn away as their faces
Fell silent again?

What had you told them
That slammed shut their looks
Like the end of a lesson
With unpopular books?
What was the writing
Which I couldn't see
As it hid between covers
And pointed at me?

Nothing much could have happened
For by the next day
We were laughing, talking,
And managed to stay
(Well, after a fashion)
Good friends for a while
But with always between us
The ghost of that smile.

# The Joke

What makes me laugh
Is when you start to tell a joke
And then forget it
Halfway through
So the joke becomes you,

Because you have always been
The biggest laugh
In my life;
It is you not doing anything by half-measure
That gives me such pleasure . . .

Like forgetting the joke
And saying *Anyway*
*What does it matter anyway?*
*But have you*
*Heard the one about . . .?*

Then you forget that too.

# *Why Did the Chicken?*

Starting out across the road
The clever little chicken slowed
Then stopped. *I'm blowed*
It clucked *if I can see*
*Why they should make a joke of me*
And turned back, very sensibly.

# FIVE ANIMAL SONGS
(adapted from the French of Robert Desnos)

## *The Owls*

The owls take a broad view:
some of them incline to
Plato, some to the new
learning – all eschew
what is suspect or untrue.

Mother owls make beau-
tiful mothers, a few
might brew more nourishing mouse stew
than they do
but most of them muddle through.

Owls' children do
as they are told, you
never get mumps or flu
if you're an owl-child nor u-
sually does the cold turn you blue.

Owls, where do you
come from? What original venue?
A bamboo
hut? An igloo?
Are you Zulu,
Eskimo, or from Peru,
Timbuctoo, Anjou,
Andalu-
sia are you?

'Too-whoo! Too-whoo!'
they answer, 'it's too
bad, but we've forgotten if we ever knew.'

## The Pelican

Captain Jonathan,
Eighteen and handsome,
Caught the first pelican
He could lay hands on,

But when Jonathan's pelican
Laid eggs for Jonathan
Out popped pelicans
Exactly like Jonathan's,

From which second pelicans'
Eggs laid for Jonathan
Out peeped a pelican
From the crack in each shell again . . .

Alas, poor Jonathan!

This could go on a long time
If you can't make omelettes.

# The Zebra

The zebra is dark and pale.
Snug behind stripes
There are no escapes:
In gaol

Is a habit with him.
He is the doomed
Beast of his mind:
He would rush back in

If you let him out.
His prison warms him. Freedom
Is not what he is about

Or the world . . .
An occasional dream
Now and then . . .
He sleeps curled

And his coat
Warms him – he bears
The print of his bars . . .

It is too late.

## The Whale

Pity the poor whale –
She is nothing at all
But nostrils and an enormous lung.
She feeds cold milk to her young.
Nevertheless, piecemeal,
She builds a whale
Nest on the ocean bed
For each huge sleepyhead.
Beneath her move
Crustaceous depths, above
The celestial foam,
The wake of liners steaming home.

# The Pike

The pike
Has journeys to make –
With a flick of his tail
He's off for the Nile
Or the Ganges
'Or' he says
'If I don't like either
There's the Tagus, the Tiber,
The Yangtze Kiang
Or . . .
What am I waiting for?'

Bursting with plans
He adjusts his fins.

And the moon, pike?
You could make it there too
Inside a week
Couldn't you?

Pike, I wish I had your go.

## Portrait

He was a cold fish:
Deeply the stillest waters
Ran beneath him
While he nibbled moonflakes
From a silver plate.

*What should I care,* he cried,
*For others in this ocean?*
*Let it be a mirror,*
*And for company the chill stars dancing*
*Or my own reflection.*

Yes, we all admired him
As we kept our distance, all
Except one huge and hungry shadow
Leaping from the depths
Which ate him whole.

## Reflections

Mirror
On the wall, is
Yours the face ill-met each
Morning? Why is it less and less
Like mine?

Keep it
(You are welcome!)
But see that it behaves.
People in glass houses shouldn't
Throw stones.

Those bags
Beneath its eyes
Are packed with weariness.
Too much overnight travelling
Caused that.

Now, though,
Is not the time
For such reflections.
Mirror, your kind was never meant
To think.

Neither
Mortal spyglass
Nor prophetic crystal –
No, you cannot tell me anything
At all.

Easy
To walk away
From mirrors, harder though
To quite forget that what's still me
Was you.

## Acrobats

I clutch your arm
You hug my shoulder.
This gets more difficult
As we grow older.

When we were young
The air was free.
Now there's a price
On you and me.

# Mickey Mouse

(a celebration of his fiftieth birthday)

Mickey Mouse is
Safe as houses,
Famous as the Empire State;
See him caper
On a paper
Napkin or a party plate.

Kids grew up with
Him like Sopwith
Camels on the Pathé News;
Hard to avoid
That celluloid
Which rocked the *Roxys* and *Bijoux*.

Now he markets
Spades and buckets,
Fizzy drinks and magazines;
A money-spinning,
Big-eared, grinning
Logo from the land of dreams.

But he survives all
Kinds of rival
And still makes it on his own;
What we love is
Mickey's movies'
Reach-me-downs which we've outgrown.

His coy grimaces
Wipe all traces
Of a shadow from our eyes;
Innocently
Heaven-bent, he
Turns the dark clouds to Blue Skies.

## Bats

Bats like various
musty old areas:

belfries, of course,
where they rehearse

a crotchety score,
dangling galore

from crossbar staves,
troubling graves

with the dark bells' boom
of their leather tune;

or a spooky loft
where dust lies soft

on forgotten things,
and someone sings

in her room below
that song bats know

whose notes contain
the squeak of pain . . .

Oh, bats like various
vicarious areas,

preferably precarious.

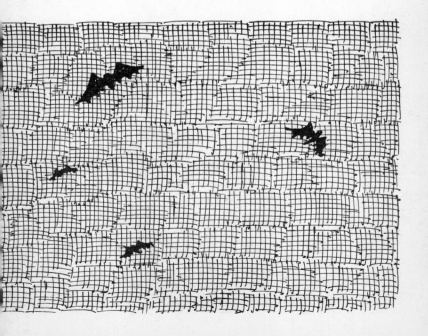

# The Box

(for Simon)

A boy lived in a cardboard box
With two holes in the lid;
Through one of them he saw each day
What other people did.

The second hole, a cross between
A chimney and a door,
Let all the outside noises in –
That's what it was for.

At night, when both the holes went dark
With nothing seen or heard,
The boy lay down on packing straw
And dreamed he was a bird;

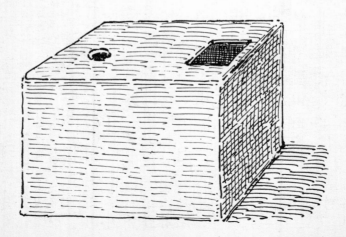

Out by the looking hole he went
To fly around till dawn,
Then back home through the listening one,
He woke up with a yawn.

And when he peered outside once more
The world was just the same
Except that someone very close
Was whispering his name –

'Oh Simon, Simon, Simon Mole
Come on, come out and play!
I'll let you be a bird by night
If you'll be my friend all day.'

## *Jack-in-the-Box*

Jack-in-the-Box is faithful,
Jack-in-the-Box is true,
But Jack-in-the-Box
Is alone in his box
And Jack-in-the-Box wants you.

Jack-in-the-Box is cunning,
Jack-in-the-Box is sly.
Can Jack-in-the-Box
Get out of his box?
Oh Jack-in-the-Box will try.

## Nowhere Bear

I'm a nowhere bear, a threadbare bear,
A ruined bruin, Monsieur Misère
With a moth-eaten coat, a buttony stare
And a bleat of a growl that's beyond repair . . .
Oh it isn't fair, it isn't fair,
I have my pride and I do still care
That I seem rather less than debonair,
So my only hope is I'll find somewhere
Before I surrender at last to despair
An old acquaintance, some kind confrère
From the days when we both had a lot more hair,
Who will take me up in his arms and declare –
You're a still very cuddly nowhere bear.

## Cat of Ages

Cat of ages
Old and new
Let me hide myself
In you

Let me listen
Through your ears
To Adam's laughter
And Eve's tears

Let me gaze
On Pharaoh's tomb
Under a high
Egyptian moon

Let me feel
My whiskers twitch
Riding a broomstick
With your witch

Let me taste
Each salty morsel
Tossed by pirates
From the fo'c's'le

Let me smell
My supper cooking
And slip back home
When you're not looking

Cat of ages
How would it be
If you hid yourself
In me?

# The Balancing Man

The balancing man
Is a diplomat;
On his cautious head
Sits a balancing hat.

Beneath that hat
I do declare
His brains are measuring
Every hair,

And every hair
Is exactly split
Into what it was
And what was it.

His smile says Now
But his eyes say When.
Never argue
With balancing men.

## Alice and Alice

Arm in arm, Alice and Alice
Have walked through the mirror on the wall
And though neither of them is pretty at all
They are both of them nice.

They are going to teach the Queen some manners,
Nobody should behave like that,
And a hatter is no excuse for his hat.
They detest caterpillars.

A race is a race. Someone must win,
And beautiful soup is a matter of taste.
When a cynical cat dissolves with such haste
It should not leave its grin.

This time the sense will take care of the sound,
Language will banish the Jabberwock,
Minutes will do as they're told by the clock
And rabbits will stay underground.

Simply begin as you mean to go on.
If the Queen should cry *Off with her head!*
Alice and Alice are well enough bred
To know two are better than one.

Croquet is played with mallet and hoops,
Flamingoes aren't held by the leg.
If you're silly enough to try mending an egg
You won't need horses and troops.

The trouble with nonsense is that it's not true
Though the bottle says *Drink me who dares.*
Common sense walks like policemen in pairs
And reason stands to.

So Alice and Alice, arm in arm,
Whom nothing shall ever put asunder,
Have set out to vanquish the forces of wonder.
They mean no harm.

# Nuncle

His party trick
Was to undo
A wooden egg
Of peacock blue

Which squeaked and scraped
Until each crown
Fell open
On an egg of brown

Which hid, as hemispheres
Enclose the dream,
Another egg
Of emerald green

Which in its turn
Et cetera . . .
What practised smartyboots
We were

To let him show them
One by one
Until the last egg
Came undone

And then –
*Nuncle, that's only half of clever!*
*Let's see you fit them*
*Back together.*

# *A Musical Family*

I can play the piano
I am nearly three.
I can play the long white note
That Mum calls Middle C.

Dad can play the clarinet.
My sister plays the fiddle,
But I'm the one who hits the piano
Slap bang in the middle.

# *Musical Chairs*

Father, weighty as a minim –
Ample the armchair that has him in.

Grandma, like a semibreve,
Rests on the couch she cannot leave.

Mother, an anxious dotted crotchet,
Out of the game, prefers to watch it.

Grandpa, a somewhat tiresome quaver,
Is hardly on his best behaviour.

Round him the children, demi-semis,
Fidget and tumble as they please.

The cat meanwhile lies fast asleep,
Oblivious of the time they keep.

# The Family Game

The game is always interrupted.
No one takes it seriously at all.
Grandpa needs to have his chair adjusted.
Mother's left her glasses in the hall.

Cousin Will keeps talking about money.
Auntie Jean can feel a nasty draught.
Grandma says it's probably the chimney.
Father thinks that Cousin Will is daft.

Mother still can't find her glasses.
Richard's making eyes at Auntie Jean.
Uncle Jack keeps talking about horses.
Grandma wonders if the chimney's clean.

Richard thinks that Auntie Jean's half-hearted.
Both of them drive Father up the wall.
I wonder how we ever got this started.
No one takes it seriously at all.

# Under the Tree

At least it's not an oven glove
*From Cynthia and Ron – with love.*

*Affectionate regards – Aunt Grace*
Something she broke and must replace.

The shop will not take this one back
*To all of you from Uncle Jack.*

*From everyone here at the Grange*
A wrong size Harrods might exchange.

Shapeless, rustling, soft and nice
*Respectfully – The Misses Price.*

*When shall I see you? Till then – Jane*
In last year's paper used again.

Under the tree, without a sound,
The parcels pass themselves around

And smile inside, not unaware
Of all the reasons they are there.

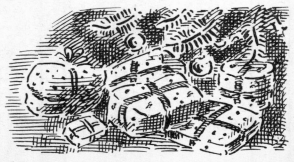

# Some More Riddles

I
Grand and solo, polished brightly,
Dance of practised fingers nightly,
Clair-de-lunar or moonlightly.

Presto, forte, pathétique,
The world is mine because I speak
A language common yet unique.

I tax to brilliant extremes
Each maestro's formalistic dreams,
All variations and all themes.

Then, when his energy withdraws
To where you sit amazed, I pause
And share with him in the applause.


2
I am the shame beneath a carpet.
No one comes to sweep me off my feet.

Abandoned rooms and unread books collect me.
Sometimes I dance like particles of light.

My legions thicken on each windowpane,
A gathering of dusk, perpetual gloom,

And when at last the house has fallen,
I am the cloud left hanging in the air.


3
Once there were dragons, with a pure flame,
And the burnt grass would always grow again.
No smoke, in those days, without a wholesome fire
Whether from good feasting or a funeral pyre.

Now there is nothing like that at all;
Man dreamed of money and he built me tall.
'More matter!' I cry, 'More matter, less art!'
And the stained plume at my tip gladdens no one's heart.


4
We rise, we fall,
Our corporation's global,
Cut-and-thrust executives
From Neptune Inc.

The world admires
Our liquid assets
And the fierce persuasion
Of our fluent tongues.

We overreach each other
In perpetual hurry;
Time is our essence
As the stocks pile high

Then, past the rocks,
Our empire crashes
At the conference table
Of a polished beach.


5
I am unnumbered rooms to explore
Or a house of correction with X on its door.

Behold the temple of place and time!
Give something a name, and it is mine.

I am the only book on your shelf
Which never quite keeps up with itself,

But if you have my revised edition
I'm *almost* the total of definition.


6
Snow-motion, lumbering
Avalanche of fur,
From my wide glass kingdom
They brought me here

To your narrow world
Where the sky is grey
And white clouds are baffled
By each gloomy day.

## *The Mad Parrot's Countdown*

10    9    Wait(!)
Pieces of 8    pieces of 8
TERMINATE
7    6    Are you still alive
My hearties?    5
Gold rings    but listen I've
Learnt more

4
(Make Love not War)
3    2
It's down to you
Yo ho ho    Yo ho WHO(?)
1
Is 1
Is a bottle of rum
And ever more shall be so
Be so    be so
Be    ZERO . . .

## Circles and Squares

Circles always meet themselves
At every turning of the way
On journeys that complete themselves
By never ending, greet themselves
Round corners then repeat themselves
Like questions. They

Are not those squares which frame themselves
From every angle that they make,
Which boastfully proclaim themselves
As always right, and name themselves
So shamelessly they shame themselves
But never notice their mistake.

# The Regretful Philosopher Apologizes to His Cat

I consider the names I did not choose
Since a kitten could hardly be thought to have views
But, now that you've grown, your widening eyes
Dilate on a world of philosophies:
Cartesian cat, your purr in the sun
Is murmuring *Cogito, ergo sum*
Or, Wittgenstein, your inscrutable face
Seems certain that everything is the case.
If this is an ideal home, you're Plato
Warming his paws in my study window
Then you make for the desk, transformed again
And, preferring the shade, become Montaigne.
When you're shut outside and it's raining hard
You look as gloomy as Kierkegaard
But on the tiles for a late-night razzle
You take hot tips from Bertie Russell.
Pensive at noon on a mellow brick wall
The secrets you keep would outblaise Pascal
Though you sometimes thump your tail, a feature
Which hints at the darker dreams of Nietzsche.
Not least, with my garden to cultivate,
Voltaire might have suited, but it's all too late
As I call you in, to my lasting shame,
By your utterly commonplace cat name.

# The Whole Duck

A duck's head under water
Is deep in thought
Which makes its body shorter
As thinking ought

Until, quick as a flash,
The whole duck reappears
And with a little splash
Floats its ideas.

## *Pig Sings*

### PIG'S SONG OF COURTSHIP

Grobble Snort
Blurp Blort
Screep Uggle
Slop Snuffle
Honk Squelch
Flubber Belch
Wee     Say
Wee     You
Wee     Love
Wee     Me

# PIG'S FAVOURITE NURSERY RHYME

Sniff Piggle Piggle
Whiff Piggle Piggle
Truffle Tum Tum
    Tump
Glop Bubble Bubble
Up Bubble Bubble
Down Derry Derry
    Dump


# PIG'S FOOTBALL CHANT

Blue Boar Kicks Mate
Who Wee Wee Appreciate?
P.I.G.
Pig!

# PIG'S LULLABY

Trouble Sorrow
Dropple Wallow
Snort Snorkle Deep
Sadly Sobble
Cradle Wobble
Sleep Sleep Sleep

## PIG'S FAREWELL

No Sow
Go Now

## Night Music

Hey diddle diddle
The Emperor's fiddle,
His soldiers are over the moon.
From andante legato
To mad pizzicato
Their wish runs away with his tune.

Where will it lead them?
He does not heed them –
Oh watch out for what music releases.
While your home is ablaze
The emperor plays
Then leaves you to pick up the pieces.

# Words of Advice from the King of Jazz

There ain't nothing worse
Than an old horn's curse.

When you try to sound slick
Them bent valves stick.

When you want to look cool
Your spit drips in a pool.

When you aim to impress
That lacquer's a mess.

When you need your tone thin
The mute won't go in.

When you're ready to shout
The mute won't come out.

But get a new horn
And, man, you're reborn.

# My Hero

Marcel Proust's my hero,
Marcel Proust's my man.
I'll tell you why
Marcel's my guy
And I'm his biggest fan.

Marcel was a writer
Who wrote his books in bed,
And no one fussed
Or said *You must
Get up, Marcel*. Instead

His friends all came to see him
And brought him special cakes;
He'd take a bite
Then start to write,
Forget his pains and aches

And murmur *I remember* . . .
The taste made him recall
A favourite game,
A flower's name,
The colour of a ball,

Until it all came pouring out.
Marcel was a *success*,
But still he lay
In bed all day
And didn't have to dress.

So that's why he's my hero –
There's homework to be done.
I didn't write
A word last night
And now the morning's come.

I'd like to lie here all day long
And try those special cakes;
I'm sure Marcel
Could count and spell
And not make bad mistakes.

Oh to be a genius,
Never to look a fool,
But best to stay
In bed all day
And not be missed at school.

## Taking the Plunge

*One day a boy said to a girl in a swimming-pool,*
*'I'm going to dive in. Are you?' She replied,*
*'No thanks. I bet you can't anyway.' So the boy*
*got on the diving-board and dived and said,*
*'See.' The girl replied, 'Flipping 'eck!'*

(Simon Wilkinson,
Margaret Wix Junior School, St Albans)

Flipping 'eck, cor blimey, 'strewth,
You're my hero, that's the honest truth.

Lumme, crikey, lordy lord,
It's a long way down from that diving-board.

Itchy beard and stone the crows,
Don't you get chlorine up your nose?

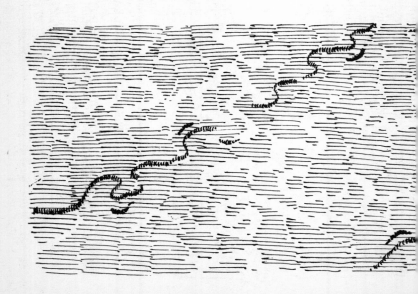

Luv a duck and strike me pink,
You're slicker than the soap in the kitchen sink.

Knock me down with a sparrow's feather,
How about us going out together?

Groovy, t'riffic, brill and smashing,
Me 'n' you, we could start things splashing.

Watcha cocky, tara, see ya,
Meet me for a Coke in the cafeteria.

Hallelujah and Amen,
If you like this poem you can read it again.

## Bank Holiday

Far beyond the dingy pier,
The derricks and the dirty boats,
Water waves her ringlets, floats
In crystal cleanliness, cool, clear,
Calm and collected. As for us, we're
Sweating on this beach, our coats
Stretched out beside us, and our throats
As tight as terror, stiff as fear.

Oh for a Coke, a ginger pop,
To touch our tongues, to lick our lips,
But all we do all day is flop
And long for breezy, tousled trips
Across the sea or dream one drop
That drips and drips and drips and drips.

## Carnival Sunday

On Carnival Sunday what could be finer
Than whanging a wellie and smashing china,

Than putting the boot in and splatting a rat
And drenching a burger with yukky tat,

Than buying old annuals you'll never read
And guessing the weight of a bear gone to seed,

Than quoiting a two-litre bottle of cola
And thumping a punch-bag which won't fall over,

Than stuffing your face until friends shout *That's
gross!*
And then fungussing it with candy-floss,

Than paying 10p for a fistful of darts
And splintering the wood round the ace of hearts,

Than junketing on an inflated castle
And not getting off when they blow the whistle,

Than watching two cars race round on a track
And cheering the one which skids on to its back,

Than raffling for a weekend in Paris for two
And wondering what, if you won, you would do,

Than finding a kid that has lost its mum
And telling the man with the microphone,

Then when it's all over what could be better
Than writing the whole world a thank-you letter?

*from* PENNY TOYS


## Sad Goose

Oh to be a swan –
I am much put upon!
Can no one transform me?
Is there no love can warm me?
Oh swan, my friend,
You will sing at the end
But I'm one of the low –
I shall just go.


## The Musical Monkey

The musical monkey is dressed like a flunkey
In bell-bottomed trousers and little peaked cap;
His master the grinder could hardly be kinder
And everyone calls him an elegant chap.
But see how his face is a world of grimaces
Which might make us wonder and should give us
pause;
Oh quaint little creature, oh great Mother Nature,
A dance for our penny, a fig for your laws.

# What Did the Pig Do?

Well, there was this show
And they had me ready to go –
Scrubbed, shiny, pink,
All that wallow, all that stink
Clean gone. I was their prize
Porker. Some size, my friends, some size!

Worth my weight, they said –
A wallet stuffed with notes, and me dead –
One of those shows where you win
*And* lose. They do you in
With one hand and pay out with the other.
Oh brother, my friends, oh brother!

So I put my feet down, all four,
When they came to get me. No more
Mucking about. You can stick your knife
Up your . . . It was *my* life
And I aimed to stay in it.
This was the limit, my friends, this was the limit!

No point being Number One
Is there, just to get done?
What I did – I leave you to guess.
There was *some* mess.
They were all thoroughly shaken
But it saved my bacon, my friends, it saved my bacon!

## The Airman's Farewell

Thanks for the spin. Don't prang the bus.
Scribbling and rhyme? No dice, old scout!
But we were the chaps. Remember us.
Willco. Roger. Over. Out.

## I am the Dog

I am the dog whose master's voice
Lifted the hearts of an Island race.

I am the dog of pluck and grit.
Nobody tells me where to sit.

I am the dog whose brave bark reaches
Bedraggled troops on foreign beaches.

I am the dog no sausage hound
Is going to budge from his native ground.

I am the dog of World War Two.
Pray tell me, sir, whose dog are you?

# Song of the Hat-raising Doll

I raise my hat
And lower it.
As I unwind
I slow a bit.
This life –
I make a go of it
But tick-tock time
I know of it.

Yes, tick-tock time
I know of it.
I fear the final
O of it,
But making
A brave show of it
I raise my hat
And lower it.

## Cinderella

It was something about
This pantomime
That puzzled me in
And out of time.

*Be back by midnight,*
*The spell can't last –*
No help from the orchestra
Or the cast.

My father holding
My mother's hand –
Why couldn't anyone
Understand?

When she reached the Ball
And danced with Prince Charming
I looked at my watch –
*It's all right, darling,*

*It's only a story*
My mother said
But the minutes ticked on
Inside my head

Until they were married,
The curtain fell,
And the future was left
To what time would tell.

# Mr Cartwright's Counting Rhyme

One, two
You, boy, yes I'm talking to you

three, four
I've wiped the floor

five, six
with others of your kind. Your tricks

seven, eight
come centuries too late

nine, ten
for experienced men

eleven, twelve
like myself

thirteen, fourteen
so just be careful to be more seen

fifteen, sixteen
than heard, or preferably not seen

seventeen, eighteen
at all. Or you could stop baiting

nineteen, twenty
and pity me.

## Buttercups
(for Hannah Chambers)

A golden boat comes sailing in,
Buttercups heaped from deck to brim
And all for a proud Babylonian king.

But Nebuchadnezzar's grizzly chin
Is thick with whiskers, the daft old thing.
What use are buttercups to him?

## Smug Jug

Though caught in the act
Of admiring itself
For its porcelain tact,
Its high-on-the-shelf
Refusal to think
That someone might dare
Ask for a drink
When seeing it there,
This jug has just proved
That a proud heart takes pains
Not to be loved
For what it contains
While a heart that is true
Though mere earthenware
Is loved through and through
For what it can pour.

# Two Songs for an Abandoned Car

1

Lie still, lie still, it all
Goes on without you
Somewhere behind another wheel
But in the same direction.

Rest, though not quite done
With never quite life –
Propped, wide-eyed
Almost skull with one door open
Like an ear listening.

2

So what do you hear?
A whisper of destinations
In the radial's tread?
So what do you hear?
A speed buffeting the wind?

Yes, and a smaller sound
Like grass, almost.
Somewhere beyond this
A man walks upright.

# *Moth*

Pity my silence pressing at your window
Frail and motionless against the night;
A baffled spectre framed by blackness,
Little moonflake, prisoner of glass.
This is my journey's end, receive me.
Brilliant keeper, rise and let me in.

Then later, when from a drawer perhaps
You take my body, wasted, brittle
As a shred of antique parchment, hold it
Gently up to the light I loved
But which bewildered me, until
I fly away again, a ghostly powder
Blown or shaken from your hand.

# Answers to the verse riddles

*A Riddle*
Telescope

*Some Riddles*
1 Stone
2 Camera
3 Snail
4 Table
5 Umbrellas
6 Leaves
7 Road
8 Apples

*Some More Riddles*
1 Piano
2 Dust
3 Factory chimney
4 Waves
5 Dictionary
6 Polar bear

# Index of first lines